Dinosaurios y animales prehistóricos/Dinosaurs and Prehistoric Animals

Tiranosaurio rex/Tyrannosaurus Rex

Edición revisada/Revised Edition

por/by Helen Frost

Traducción/Translation: Dr. Martín Luis Guzmán Ferrer

Editor Consultor/Consulting Editor: Dra. Gail Saunders-Smith

Consultor/Consultant: Jack Horner, Curator of Paleontology
Museum of the Rockies
Bozeman, Montana

CAPSTONE PRESS
a capstone imprint

Pebble Plus is published by Capstone Press,
1710 Roe Crest Drive, North Mankato, Minnesota 56003.
www.mycapstone.com

Library of Congress Cataloging-in-Publication Data is available on the Library of Congress website.

ISBN: 978-1-5157-6178-5 (revised paperback)
ISBN: 978-1-5157-6179-2 (ebook pdf)

Summary: Simple text and illustrations present sabertooth cats, their body parts, and behavior—in both
English and Spanish.

Editorial Credits
Martha E. H. Rustad, editor; Katy Kudela, bilingual editor; Eida del Risco, Spanish copy editor; Linda Clavel,
set designer; Jon Hughes, illustrator; Wanda Winch, photo researcher; Scott Thoms, photo editor

Photo Credit
Jon Hughes, Cover, 1, 5, 7, 9, 11, 13, 15, 17, 19
Shutterstock: Vlad G, 21

**The author thanks the children's library staff at the Allen County Public Library in Fort Wayne, Indiana,
for research assistance.**

Note to Parents and Teachers

The Dinosaurios y animales prehistóricos/Dinosaurs and Prehistoric Animals set
supports national science standards related to the evolution of life. This book describes
sabertooth cats in both English and Spanish. The images support early readers in
understanding the text. The repetition of words and phrases helps early readers learn
new words. This book also introduces early readers to subject-specific vocabulary words,
which are defined in the Glossary section. Early readers may need assistance to read
some words and to use the Table of Contents, Glossary, Internet Sites, and Index sections
of the book.

Table of Contents

Tabla de contenidos

A Tall Dinosaur

Tyrannosaurus rex

was a tall dinosaur

with big teeth.

Un dinosaurio muy alto

El tiranosaurio rex era

un dinosaurio muy alto

con dientes muy grandes.

4

Tyrannosaurus rex lived
in prehistoric times. It lived
about 70 million years ago
in western North America.

El tiranosaurio rex vivió en
la era prehistórica. Vivió hace
cerca de 70 millones de años en
el oeste de América del Norte.

How Tyrannosaurus Rex Looked

Tyrannosaurus rex was
as tall as an elephant.
It was about 12 feet
(4 meters) tall.

Cómo eran los tiranosaurios rex

El tiranosaurio rex era tan alto
como un elefante. Medía cerca
de 4 metros (12 pies) de alto.

Tyrannosaurus rex
had a thick neck
and a large head.

El tiranosaurio rex tenía
el cuello grueso y
una enorme cabeza.

Tyrannosaurus rex
had short arms
and sharp claws.

El tiranosaurio rex tenía
las patas cortas y
las garras muy afiladas.

What Tyrannosaurus Rex Did

Tyrannosaurus rex

walked and ran

on its long, strong legs.

Qué hacían los tiranosaurios rex

El tiranosaurio rex caminaba

y corría con sus largas y

fuertes patas.

14

Tyrannosaurus rex
used its long tail
for balance.

El tiranosaurio rex
usaba su cola para
mantener el equilibrio.

Tyrannosaurus rex hunted
and ate other animals.
It also ate animals
that were already dead.

El tiranosaurio rex cazaba a
otros animales y se los comía.
También comía animales que
ya estaban muertos.

The End of Tyrannosaurus Rex

Tyrannosaurus rex died out
about 65 million years ago.
No one knows why they all died.
You can see tyrannosaurus rex fossils
in museums.

El fin del tiranosaurio rex

El tiranosaurio rex desapareció hace
cerca de 65 millones de años. Nadie
sabe por qué todos murieron. Se pueden
ver fósiles de tiranosaurios rex en
los museos.

Glossary

balance—to counter the weight of something; tyrannosaurus rex used the weight of its tail to balance the weight of its head and upper body.

claw—a hard curved nail on the foot of an animal or bird

dinosaur—a large reptile that lived on land in prehistoric times

fossil—the remains or traces of an animal or a plant, preserved as rock

museum—a place where interesting objects of art, history, or science are shown

North America—the continent in the Western Hemisphere that includes the United States, Canada, Mexico, and Central America

prehistoric—very, very old; prehistoric means belonging to a time before history was written down.

Glosario

América del Norte—continente en el Hemisferio Occidental que incluye los Estados Unidos, Canadá, México y Centroamérica

el dinosaurio—reptil grande de la prehistoria que vivía en tierra

el equilibrio—compensar el peso de algo; el tiranosaurio rex usaba el peso de su cola para equilibrar el peso de su cabeza y la parte superior del cuerpo.

el fósil—restos o vestigios de un animal o una planta que se conservan como piedras

la garra—uña dura y curva en la pata de un animal o un pájaro

el museo—lugar donde se exhiben objetos de arte, historia o ciencias

prehistórico—muy, muy viejo; prehistórico quiere decir perteneciente a una época antes de que hubiera historia escrita.

Internet Sites

FactHound offers a safe, fun way to find Internet sites related to this book. All of the sites on FactHound have been researched by our staff.

Here's how:

1. Visit *www.facthound.com*

2. Choose your grade level.

3. Type in this book ID **0736866884** for age-appropriate sites. You may also browse subjects by clicking on letters, or by clicking on pictures and words.

4. Click on the **Fetch It** button.

FactHound will fetch the best sites for you!

Sitios de Internet

FactHound proporciona una manera divertida y segura de encontrar sitios de Internet relacionados con este libro. Nuestro personal ha investigado todos los sitios de FactHound. Es posible que los sitios no estén en español.

Se hace así:

1. Visita *www.facthound.com*

2. Elige tu grado escolar.

3. Introduce este código especial **0736866884** para ver sitios apropiados según tu edad, o usa una palabra relacionada con este libro para hacer una búsqueda general.

4. Haz clic en el botón **Fetch It**.

¡FactHound buscará los mejores sitios para ti!